I0423221

THE HUSBAND'S TEXTBOOK

52 Lessons

BOB BRYAN

The Husband's Textbook: 52 Lessons
By Bob Bryan

DEDICATION

This book is dedicated to my first love,
my wife of 48 wonderful years.
She and the Lord have shaped me
and inspired this book.

CONTENTS

My hope and prayer is that
the bits of wisdom written in this book
will help many married men to understand
some ways to improve the relationships with
their wives, which will result in
a happier marriage.

FACTS VS. EMOTIONS

Facts (husbands) vs. Emotions and Intuition (wives). The facts are that your wife has more emotions that are just as real and strong as your facts. So consider that there could be two sides to the story. Have you considered what is called compromise – a give and take? You could both come out winners and friends rather than reach a standoff.

Men are slow to realize that they don't usually have as strong emotions as a woman. What, to a man, is the most important are facts, as he sees them and tries to get his wife to understand them. In reality, the fact is that his wife's emotions and feelings are also important and may be more so.

To most men, emotions are childish and not manly. This belief is slowly changing in today's society. Men are coming to feel that tears are ok and even humility is a desirable quality.

Facts are still important and the wife may even sometimes give in, but don't expect it or push it. Don't gloat if you do win. At best, don't let her see you smile.

The bottom line is that your wife has a side that a computer can't understand.

TIED UP OR TANGLED UP

There is a difference between being tied up in a knot and being tangled up. It is easier to get a knot untied, but when you are tangled up you are in a mess.

You can be tangled up and not even realize anything is wrong. Many a husband thought everything was all right between him and his woman until it was too late. What you think is a slipknot may turn out to be a noose.

Getting tangled up is easy to do, but getting untangled is a lot harder and requires some determined concentration. A man never starts out to get tangled up but it can happen slowly over time.

A little secret here and then another, and you convince yourself that you didn't cross the line but the line was a rope and you got caught. Beware of a snare in your path.

This is where morals can come into play. Remember to keep your marriage vows, perhaps a framed copy hanging in your bedroom. Throw in the Golden Rule and you will be a lot less likely to become so tangled up that the marriage knot won't become a slip knot.

TOGETHER

Do it together...eat, sleep, cook, pray, read and exercise.

Family meals together at the same time of day help maintain family stability and communications. "Non functional families" are the opposite. They don't do things together. Turn off the TV, phone and music and have some time for family togetherness. Read, talk, sing, exercise, play games, manicure each other's nails, massage feet, neck or back. Clean house, wash the car, look at old photographs, plan vacations, start a hobby, and set goals. Do go to bed at the same time as she does. Don't have a TV in your bedroom; that's not what the bedroom is for.

Spend as much quality time together as possible. After all, isn't that why you got married? The girls' night out and/or the boys' night out should be a thing of the past or very, very limited. Go to church together.

One thing that you should consider doing separately on some occasions is to visit your family without her and she visits hers without you. Parents enjoy having their son or daughter back for a short stay. But don't get use to being spoiled.

WATER

Clear, pure, clean water is an element that the human body must have on a regular basis in order to stay healthy. Some people don't drink enough water causing their body to suffer in several ways because of that lack.

Clean water can also become easily polluted. It can become muddy, cloudy, or bad tasting. Unhealthy organisms and drought can dry it up.

Marriage needs clean, pure, abundant love just like the body needs clean, abundant water. Just like a drought; love can dry up. Just like clean water, love can become polluted and unhealthy. Just as a body without water cannot survive, neither will a marriage without love.

A marriage that is clean, clear and unpolluted is a healthy marriage. Infidelity, bad habits, weak communication and even family and friends are some broad areas that can contaminate your marriage.

As a stone thrown into a pond creates ripples causing a reaction in the rest of the pond, everything that affects you will also affect your family. You can't say, "I'm not hurting anybody but myself." Ask yourself this question, "Would I want what I'm doing to be published in the local newspaper?"

GREEN GRASS?

How green is your grass? Is the grass really greener on the other side of the fence? Remember the side of the fence that you are on is the one of your own choosing.

The grass on the other side of the fence may look more desirable, but it will leave a bad taste in your mouth and give you an upset stomach if partaken of.

Watch out when you decide to jump the fence or just stick your neck through for a nibble. There are barbs and possible electricity on the fence. So be wary that while you are checking out someone else's grass, someone may be looking over your fence.

If your grass is no longer as green as it used to be, then invest in restoring it. You will find that by keeping attention on your own grass, efforts and thoughts will be channeled in the right direction. Your grass (wife) may need some encouragement, flattery or a new "make-over". Do whatever is needed in order to have a wife that will help keep your eyes off the neighbor's grass.

Don't be bull headed and go astray.

TRANSPARENT

You are a ghost! I mean people can see right through you. You are not fooling anybody, especially your wife. She knows what you are really like. The only one deceived is you. Just stand in front of a mirror and be truthful with yourself about what you see.

While you look at your physical shape, try to imagine four of you. There is a mental you, a spiritual you and an emotional you along with the physical. Ask yourself how big and strong each is. Which one needs the most help?

The mental you, of course, deals with your mind. Do you write? Do you read? You need to do these in addition to your job. Try keeping a journal.

For the emotional, you can use some quiet time…a time to relax and release any tension.

The spiritual you is the key to who you really are and is not fully understood with your mind or emotions. You are not the person you can or should be without this part.

Where should you go to get the help you need? All four of you are important and need daily exercise in order to stay healthy. You may think you are a real man if you can raise a bicep, but your real strength is a well rounded and complete four.

REPAIRS

What condition is your house in? What condition is your home in? NO! They are not the same and their condition is rarely the same. Your house could be a show place and everything in tip-top working order. However, your home may be falling apart.

The windows in your house may not be cracked or broken, but in the home your wife's heart may be broken and you haven't even tried to fix it.

The things in your house are up-to-date and new, but in your home your love life is not fresh, young and what it used to be. The alarm system on your house will sound loud and clear when trouble comes, but can you hear the alarm going off in your home?

It is easy to pay an electrician, plumber, or carpenter to repair your house, but who do you pay to fix your home life?

Fixing broken relationships in your home is usually a lot more complicated and time consuming than repairs on your house, so how about putting into practice the advice given in this book?

The condition of the home is always the more important and takes more up-keep.

WHAT LIST?

What is on your "to-do" list? I'm not talking about the "honey-do" list your wife made for you and keeps adding to. I'm talking about the one you created for yourself. You do have one, don't you?

Where is it? When did you see it last, go over it and update it? A husband needs to have a list of things that he wants to do, and he needs to go over this list with his wife.

This is not just to get her O.K., but for her to see what your needs and desires and goals are. The wife should share her list also. This way you can both be on the same page as far as recreation, entertainment, activities, long range goals, things to buy or sell, hobbies, vacations, etc.

Some of the things on your list may not interest her. That's understandable, because some of her list will not be of interest to you. This is OK as long as it is agreeable with each of you. Look at your list again and put a star beside the things that are most important to you. Also include on your list the things that you and she can do together. HAVE FUN!

THE STRENGTH OF A MAN

Just how strong of a man are you? We're not really asking about your biceps. How will you be able to face the real challenges that come into every person's life at some time or another?

Perhaps your health has a serious problem. Can you handle it emotionally, mentally, and spiritually? Your finances get out of your control. Are you humble enough to live on less and work for less?

What about the loss of loved ones. Are you strong enough to reach out to comfort others with love and compassion as well as receive it back?

If you live long enough, sooner or later something will come along that will hit you hard. How will you react? Will you lie down and give up? Don't do that and don't leave your wife out of the solution. These are times when you really need each other for comfort, support and advice. Make plans to overcome.

There is no weakness in asking for help when facing any type of need. We all need each other. Macho can be a weakness, not a strength.

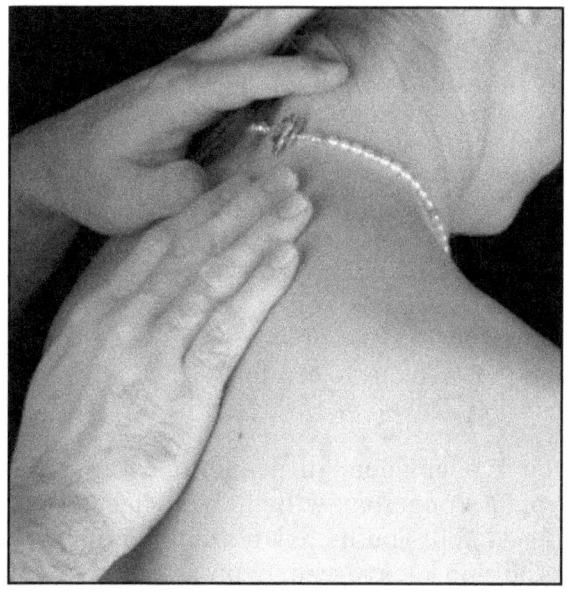

QUALITIES OF A GOOD HUSBAND

What are the qualities of a good husband?

1. A good sense of humor. Make her laugh as often as you can. Women like a man who shows a good sense of humor.

2. Pay attention to her in a group, not just at home. Show some affection in public; this will add points to your credit. Be a gentleman... open the door, let her go first, don't walk ahead, hold hands frequently, and put your arm around her when sitting beside her.

3. Be a caregiver at home. Massage her feet with lotion. File her toenails. Massage her shoulders and back. Help with household chores like dishes, vacuuming, and cleaning windows, and yes, even the bathroom.

4. Do things that make her proud to say, "That's my husband." Don't look like a slob.

5. Do something that will amaze her. Keep her in the loop, as you are undertaking a project to make sure that you have her understanding. Build onto the house, invent something, learn a new language, or climb Mt. Everest. In your dreams!!

RAINY DAY SAVINGS

Save up some money for a rainy day. Oh, yes, but you had better have a stash of cash for her special days. What days? Valentines, Anniversaries, Birthdays and why not Mother's Day? And I know you will spend a lot for Christmas.

What you can do on these special occasions depends on how much you can afford to spend and on your imagination and planning. Romance, think romance! Think privacy. Think luxury.

What size of clothes does she wear? Write it down and put it in your wallet beside of your green backs. What is her favorite color? Perfume?

You need to have those dates memorized and be prepared ahead of time with a card and whatever else you think she would like. Now about the card... don't just sign it "Love, your husband." Write some sweet, personal, humorous words inside. Maybe even add something green also.

Here are some things not to get her. Pots and pans, vacuum cleaners, a set of scales, diet books, Bengay, a girdle or breath mints. And lingerie and thongs are really not for her, are they?

DOG HOUSE AND / OR HOT WATER

When you mess up, and you will or at least your wife may think so, what do you do? Well, the natural and manly thing to do is to defend yourself. Argue your point, state the facts, or hire a lawyer.

This may sound like good advice, but it usually doesn't work with wives. Have you ever heard of pleading guilty and throwing yourself on the mercy of the court? Try this...stand in front of a mirror and repeat these statements until you can say them without laughing or stuttering.

"I am sorry. I was wrong. You were right. Will you please forgive me? I'll be careful not to let it happen again. I love you so much."

It may help to think of something else while you are reciting your speech. Perhaps think of a time when you really were wrong. Perhaps you could be thinking of something more pleasant than eating crow.

Now this won't come easy for you. Saying this is hard enough but meaning it is even more difficult. But you can do it! Try it, you'll like it!

MANY HATS

Your wife – what is she worth to you? How much would you have to pay for a good cook, a merry maid, a nurse, a secretary or a counselor? How much would it cost you to have a personal shopper, an interior decorator, or someone to do the laundry?

Most wives do at least all of these jobs. Some do even more, such as being a barber, a butler, a chauffeur, a gardener, a bookkeeper, a telephone operator, an income provider, a social planner, to name a few more. And she does all this with patience, compassion and love.

And what do you pay her for all this? If a husband had to hire all of this work done for him, most of us could not come close to affording it.

I didn't even mention what most husbands get from their wives, because that is too personal and intimate. It's not a legal job that comes with sincerity. At least learn to say "Thank you" and "I appreciate that."

If you are blessed to have a good wife, then you will learn, as time goes on, that the love you had for her has grown and now includes things like appreciation and admiration for the person that she is and how fortunate you are to be able to really say "I LOVE YOU".

GETTING AND GIVING

Getting and giving! Don't expect to get the getting before giving the giving. If you want some loving, then expect it to cost you something. That doesn't necessarily mean money, although that helps to sweeten the pot.

It also means kindness ("Thank you, dear"), compliments,("Wow, you look good"), helping ("Here, let me do that for you"), fun ("What would you like to do?") , caring ("Here is a gift certificate to the spa."), sharing, ("Here is half of the income tax refund for you"), listening, ("I hear that and you are right") and communication, ("Honey can we really afford for me to have that?")

These are some ways to build up points that can be used to get. However, points can be subtracted easier than they can be added.

Ways to lose points: Criticizing and/or contradicting, especially in front of others. Revealing private matters is a loss. Anything that you do or say that degrades your wife makes you look bad and wipes away any good you did.

DID YOU PUT THE TOILET SEAT
BACK DOWN?? POINTS!!

BIRDS & BEES AND SKUNKS & FLEAS

What are little boys made of? What animal would your wife say you are most like?

A Lamb? Gentle and easy to lead wherever she wants to go. Are you a wolf in sheep's clothing? You can't be trusted; you are two faced and deceitful.

A Chameleon? Able to adapt and change as necessary or blend in and avoid conflict.

A Deer? – Harmless, but cautious.

A Sloth? – Slow but patient and will eventually get the job done if left alone.

A Caterpillar? – Not much to begin with, but now through metamorphosis has turned into a beautiful butterfly and the sky is the limit.

A Rabbit? – Slam bam thank you maam.

A Monkey? – Looks and acts somewhat like a man.

A Dog? Have you learned how to follow orders and be obedient? How good are you at begging for your treat?

YOU ANIMAL!

BOXING GLOVES

Confrontations vs. disagreements. A disagreement is a difference of opinion on anything. This is usually easily settled. All you need to do in these cases is to say, "Yes dear." You can feel as if you have won because you got in the last word.

Now confrontations are a different level and you don't want to go there. Whoever said "no pain, no gain" wasn't talking about a confrontation between a husband and a wife. A confrontation is going to cause pain. That pain never goes away and it hurts both of you for a long time, in memories, emotions, and feelings.

Avoid a confrontation at all costs. Nobody wins and it can be deadly to a marriage. Never disagree unless in private. And don't go to bed mad at each other.

The way to avoid a confrontation is to "nip it in the bud" or in other words, don't let something small grow into an uncontrollable problem. Don't think she will forget about it or it's no big deal or the problem will just go away in time. One big confrontation and you lose all your points. That's just the least of it. A confrontation can be a knockout punch, so duck!

MAN OR WIMP

A man can get in touch with his feminine side and still be a man. This doesn't mean he needs to become a wimp. His wife doesn't really want that in a husband.

It does mean to consider her point of view; you know that she thinks with both sides of her brain and you with only one side. Also, it does not mean that just because you are a man, you can be forceful or bullying to get control.

Don't be a wimp, but don't let her control go too far. Only you know how much is too much. This is an individual decision. You need to draw a line and let her know when she gets close to crossing it.

Anyone will push you as far as you will let him or her, including your wife.

Being a man means that at some point in a situation you have got to stand up for yourself. You have certain rights and at some point you may have to assert yourself. Don't worry too much about this because you will know when that point is reached. The shock to you will be when you realize that people will admire you more.

MONEY, HONEY?

Money! This is something that should have been discussed and hopefully decided on before you got married. The matter of whoever controls money in a marriage is a major hurdle to cross and has tripped up many a couple and caused a lot of bruised feelings and egos.

Money disputes have caused problems in most marriages. Handling the family income is a big responsibility. It takes time, accuracy, patience and that is just when everything is going smoothly. Whoever is the bookkeeper in the family, you or wife, needs the trust and gratitude from the other, as it is a big task. Advice:

1. Don't count your money until it is in your hand.

2. Better to stay away from "get rich quick" schemes. A savings account is a more sure idea.

A man should have some money in his pockets to feel like he can buy whatever he wants. Lunch, chewing gum and mints are not extravagant purchases and should not break the budget.

The worth of man is not really how many green backs he can flash. When asking your wife for some money, don't be greedy. Start small and ask for pocket change. It is better than having no money at all.

More advice... Don't try to tell her how much you are worth; you might end up with nothing but a low self-esteem.

GET IN STEP

Lead, follow, or be stuck together. Which pace is the best for a man and a wife? In some marriages a man can become very successful in his occupation and get the feeling that he has "outgrown" his wife.

I will call this being in the lead. The role can be reversed and the wife takes the lead and the man is the follower. In either case it usually ends with each going his/her own separate way.

So is stuck together the way to live? Not necessarily. This usually means that one or each has a short leash around their necks. So what is the distance that works best? Each one needs some space.

It is good to have a marriage where there is enough trust to let the other have some freedom to plan activities apart from the spouse. There are no set rules for this but each person (wife and husband) needs to feel fulfilled in their life style.

Each needs some control over their life. Each needs to have a life that does not depend totally on the other. Get a life!

BAGGAGE CHECK

A husband's baggage! What did you have before you "got hitched?" Pals or buddies? You probably still remember some of their names. They probably still exist, but you are no longer in their circle.

Buddies, pals and friends; this is some of the baggage that you leave at the altar. Does this mean that you no longer have friends? Not necessarily. New friends are what you acquire now. They come out of the woodwork or more like from your wife's friends' husbands.

Try to learn their names; that's so your friends can at least put a face with the name. Smile and act friendly. They usually don't bite and they are there for the same reason you are. Their wives set all this up so that you could meet your new pals, buddies, and friends.

Wives usually plan the social gatherings and you should be grateful that she does. Otherwise, you would just stay home with your feet propped up watching a football game on television. You can erase that awful image from your mind because most wives don't go for football. They are socially oriented and incline to make you socially acceptable. Who's who?

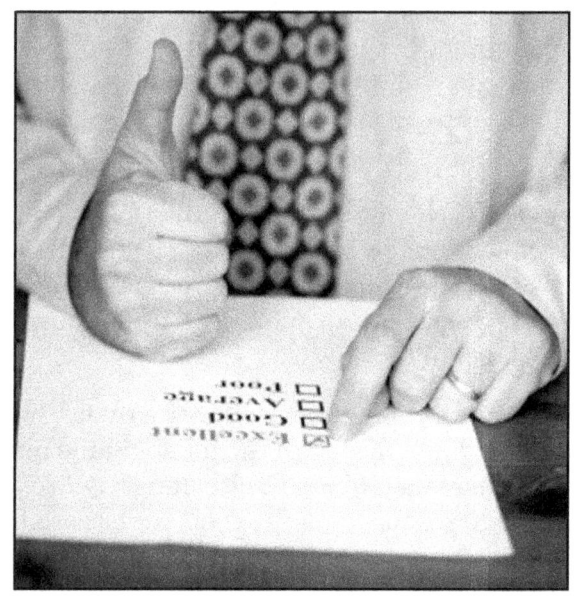

PASS OR FAIL

Have you ever stopped to wonder why she consented to take you as a husband? She took on a large task. Training you will most likely take a long time and use up most of her patience.

Let's see what she is working with. Do the terms "hard headed" or "stubborn" ring a bell? She first has to break your will. She may try to motivate you sometimes with praise for doing it right or give you a prize. Normally the higher you jump, the better the prize.

Sometimes you may forget what she thought you had learned; no prize. There are some lessons that are more important than others and so you had better learn them fast.

Don't worry about which ones they are. Your teacher will make sure you understand them. It is not a question of will you learn to be the kind of husband she wants, but rather, how fast you catch on. Don't think that "not listening" or "going in one ear and out the other" or "playing dumb" or "two rams butting heads together" will change the outcome. You are hitched. That means that you are the work horse and she controls the reins. Be the teacher's pet!

CHILL OUT

Anger Management 101 – first thing is to turn down the voice volume control knob. This means *your knob* because this is not the time to be touching any of her knobs.

Raising your voice is a sign of anger and frustration. This means that you are losing control of your emotions. You need to get your anger under control because raising your voice is only the beginning of what can follow.

Hitting something or someone can physically harm yourself or your wife or both. This will leave permanent, physical and psychological scars. Throwing things can also stem from anger. This causes damage to your property. Don't let your anger get that far. *Cool It!*

Getting angry will probably happen on occasion, which is not the problem. The problem is learning to control your anger so that it is released slowly and controlled in privacy. You don't want to wind up in jail. Control your road rage because I am on the road also.

MAN OR MACHINE

A real man is not supposed to cry, so we are told. I know most boys were taught that. They were told "suck it up; you are a big boy." Men have always been brought up believing that displaying emotions shows weakness.

"Hold it in, don't let it out," especially in public. Feelings are hard for most men to even talk about much less to express or understand them. Men are usually inadequate in knowing what to do when their wife displays some kind of emotion.

Men feel uncomfortable when emotions are being shown. Men do not discuss emotional topics when they are together. Women do!

A husband who has and will show emotions is a more complete man. Most people are attracted to a person who show love or sorrow, pain or joy, sadness or excitement. Showing your emotions is another way of letting people know just how you feel.

A man is not a complete man until he has emotions and feelings and feels free to let them out. Your wife will have more man than a mannequin.

POSITIVE OUTLOOK

Bad times and good times. Good times; not a problem. Hopefully every couple will enjoy lots of good times, but what about those other times.

Those times when an unexpected event comes along that sets you back or even throws you for a loop. These are the times that test what kind of a man or husband you are.

These are the times that test a marriage. Any family can handle the good times, but the bad times can be good times too. A lot depends on your attitude and just how you will handle and how you will come through these problems.

You can become better or become bitter. You can become stronger or broken. You can decide to be together or farther apart. Bad times come to us all in some form or another.

Bad times don't have to last; they can be overcome. Think positive and good thoughts. Get all the help you can.

You may not be the one facing a bad time. It may be a friend or family member. This is an opportunity to offer help. This gives that person encouragement and an outsider's perspective regarding the situation. Offering your resources to others will come back to you someday.

ROOMMATES

Is a "love nest" the way you would describe your home life? What are the things going on in your "love nest?" She can be seen sitting on his lap with their arms around each other. They kiss for no apparent reason. They may pillow fight or wrestle. They may do silly things together, like go to bed before bedtime.

But a "love nest" can slowly fade into a memory, as a couple becomes just two people living in the same house. They may now each have their own bedroom. The reason, he snores or some other excuse, will justify their actions.

They may each have their own T.V. room and the only way for her to get through to the husband is to stand in her birthday suit in front of his T.V.

They still love and care for each other, but are now merely doing their own thing. What has happened? Is this what you have to look forward to? The first step to fixing the situation is to realize that a problem exists. The problem usually comes as a gradual change. Second step may be to see your doctor for any physical help. Third step is to revert back to the way things use to be in the original love nest. Put some spark back into something besides the fireplace!

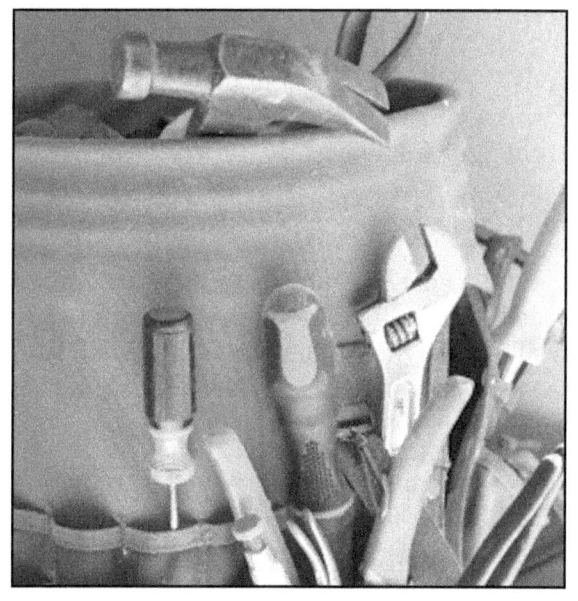

OUTER SPACE

Space! Husbands need a little space to call their own. This space could be small or large. That all depends on what your wife will agree to or let you have.

Space No. 1 is in the bathroom. When you've got to go, then lock the door.

Space No. 2 is your wallet; hers is her pocketbook. This is out of respect for each other's space.

Space No. 3 is your tools. The wife needs to ask permission for whatever she may need and to make sure she returns the tool to its rightful space ASAP.

Space No. 4 is at least a table and chair where you can read or write or draw or build and keep some files or calendar. This is not for the Internet. The Internet should be in a space that is open to everyone in the home.

Space No. 5 is a "man cave" and should be called a "game room" or a "video room". This should be open to everyone in the family. This space should be off limits to the telephone and space No. 4. This space could include some exercise equipment and/ or refreshments. This is a noisy place and is not conducive to reading, studying, or homework. It can look like a man cave. That's okay.

KNOWLEDGE BASE

Here are some things to know and remember.

What is the truth? It is whatever your wife says it is.

It is better to be loved than to know who is right.

The old saying "it's the thought that counts" is not enough when it comes to being special to her. At that time you need to think big and do big. Don't just think, do.

Security is important to a wife. So get in the habit of locking all the doors and keep an eye on her pocketbook.

Secrets are best kept. Your wife's age is best you forget and don't discuss it with anyone. Hair color and weight or dress size…. Hush!

Time is a relative thing when on the phone. To your wife time on the phone was only a few minutes, but the clock moved an hour.

Don't be surprised at what you don't know. After all she's told you at least a dozen times.

"I knew that!"

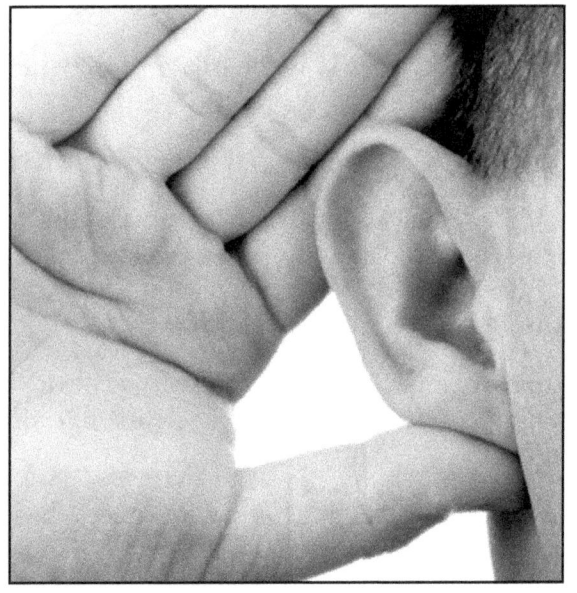

A+ OR F-

What's what? The answer to this question eludes many husbands. When you can't seem to understand your wife, or what is happening between the two of you, you are too busy to see the whole picture. You may not know what is the most important answer to your needs and desires in the marriage relationship.

Here is the answer. Love your wife. Put her needs and desires as important as your needs and desires. *What* you give out is *what* you get back. That's the answer to <u>what's what</u>! Give her all of you – your ears, your eyes, your hands and especially your time. When you do these things you are paying yourself untold benefits.

This is like putting money in the bank and letting it earn interest. If you were asked to rate your marriage relationship on a scale from 0 to 100 with 100 being the goal to reach, would you have a passing score or have you failed? What could you do to raise your score? Were you truly honest in your evaluation or just hopeful? How did your score compare with your wife's? And now you know.

JOB DESCRIPTION

How to do. Husbands will learn how to do more than he thought a man needed to know. I have heard some husbands make a statement "that's woman's work."

That remark was made before he became "domesticated." What can fit your hand besides the remote control? The vacuum cleaner is not as much fun to run as the riding mower, but you might as well learn to like it. A rag can be just a rag for cleaning the grease off your hands after working on the car or cleaning the grease from the dishes in the kitchen sink.

Some other handles to get acquainted with are: broom, mop, scrub brush and potato peeler. If you don't place your fingers around those items, then don't be surprised when there is nothing prepared there for the spoon and fork that you have in your hand.

Being domesticated also includes such things as putting your clothes away (not on the floor or wherever), helping make the bed, serving yourself coffee, fetching your own slippers, newspaper, etc. Have you learned about the controls on the washer, dryer, dishwasher, and the microwave? The T.V. remote is not the only tool in the house.

Can you handle it?

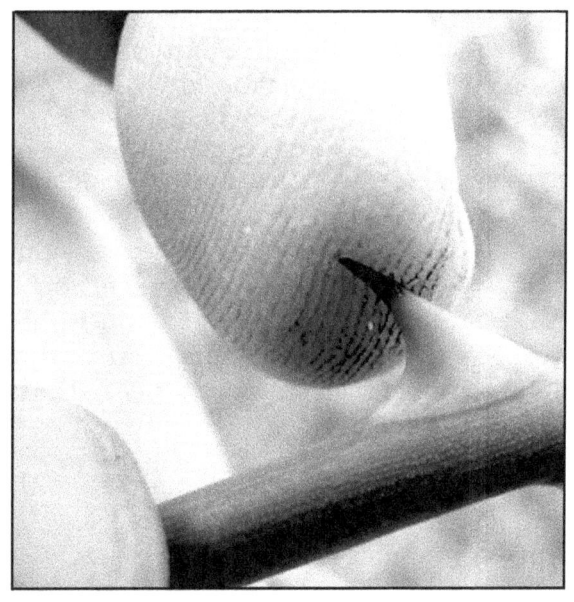

GRAVEL AND THORNS

Small Stuff! I know you have heard the saying "don't sweat the small stuff." Well, when it comes to a marriage relationship that advice doesn't hold true. There is no such thing in your partnership as "small stuff."

You may have also heard the saying, "nip it in the bud." This is the advice to go by in dealing with little disagreements that can arise from time to time.

To you as the "man of the house" it may not be anything to be concerned about, but to the "person in charge," it may be a "5 alarm fire" situation. It is easier to handle a small problem than one that has grown out of hand and be impossible to control. What is going to make both of you happy?

That gravel in your shoe can feel like a boulder and cause damage. A mole hill can become a mountain. What are some small things: The T.V. is too loud (she can't talk on the phone). Don't move anything (she knows if something has changed). She says, "That looked like an interesting place back there". (Just proceed to make a legal U-turn). She says, "I have to see about everything!" (You had better ask, "What have I not done now?" Remember the best advice is "If mama ain't happy, ain't nobody happy."

SHE REMEMBERS

Bite your tongue! That is good advice when speaking to your wife and especially if there is anyone else to hear what you are saying. Just because you say, "I'm sorry, please forgive me" a hundred times doesn't erase those hurtful words.

Just because you "think" something, doesn't mean that you have to "say" it. Think before you speak so that your mouth can produce "kind" words.

Kind words will keep you out of hot water and the doghouse, and will build up points. Remember once those words are out, you can't take them back. Wives don't forget and they don't let you forget.

However, when you are confronted, don't back up and walk away. Don't shut up; it is better to talk, talk, talk, but choose your words carefully and don't raise your voice. Stay calm and loving.

Communication is a key factor in your marriage. Don't make assumptions and expect to read each other's minds. It's good to share your thoughts with her. Discuss concerns as they happen. Don't allow them to pile up and then try to resolve them at one sitting. These confrontations could result to marriage counseling or worse.

WHAT AND WHAT NOT

What not to say is as important as what to say. Encouragement is better than criticizing. Women in general are self-conscious about their looks so don't be critical.

Snoring problems? Just wear ear plugs. Leg hair and toenails are a couple of "keep mouth shut" topics. Wear long pants to cover the scratches unless they require stitches. Some things are not worth our getting upset or aggravated or argumentative about, so let it go.

A lot of things will take care of themselves sooner or later. Some things, the more you stir and poke, the worse it stinks. Her cooking is another area to be careful of what you say or don't say. It might be beneficial to watch your facial expressions. Comparison to your mom's cooking will only lead to heartburn.

Your wife's driving may have you gripping the seat belt, but don't let her see you sweat. Turn up the A.C. and check your insurance policy.

What not to say when first arriving home: "Has anybody called?" or "Has anybody been here?", or "What's for supper? I'm starved!" That's called getting started off on the wrong foot.

What do you say? "Honey, it is so good to come home to you! I've missed and thought about you all day. Would you like to go out to dinner or are we going to enjoy one of your awesome meals?" Watch what you say. This is another opportunity to keep your foot out of your mouth.

OUTLAWS AND INLAWS

When you asked for her hand in marriage you may not have realized at the time, but there were other hands that came along with hers. Some call them in-laws; some think of them as extra baggage, but whatever they are called, they are part of the marriage deal.

They are not all compatible with each other, much less with you and the in-laws that are on your side of the family. That mix can become a mass of personalities and emotions.

There will ensue a pecking order to see who is the most important and right on down the scale. Where do you stand in all of this? As a husband, your first obligation is to honor your wife and expect others to honor her as well. It may be up to you to see to it that your side of the family gets equal treatment as does your wife's family. Be fair and equal with your time, activities and gifts to both sides of the family.

Your next role is to keep peace in the family. Watch what you say and to whom you say it. If you can't say something good about your in-laws then it's all right to be quiet or to exaggerate a little.

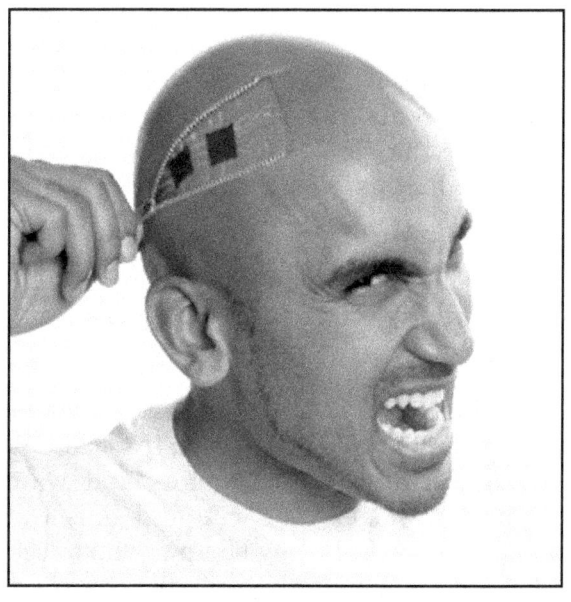

COMPUTER VS. MIND

Computers have come a long way in helping a person analyze and organize and communicate. Computers have changed the educational classroom and homework setup.

How do computers operate? You know the answer. Someone has to program them and then reprogram them or add to their program. Your mind is similar to a computer in that it can store and analyze facts. Your mind can be added to and even be reprogrammed.

However, reprogramming your mind can run into resistance from your own mind. The mind says "yes" to the things that bring pleasure. Your mind resists the thoughts of undoing what your body and mind have enjoyed in the past.

The mind needs help to change. You must limit your access to the pleasure. Get your mind, body and time involved in other things. Out of your mouth comes what is implanted in your mind, so if hatred is in, hatred comes out; however, if love is in, love comes out. Lust in, lust out.

Program your mind with worthwhile information, not trash. You will stay out of trouble and naturally make points.

Does that compute?

SECURITY

What does she want from you really? Is it love and affection? Some want love and affection and you hope so. But fellows, here is something that is also important to a wife that you may not have realized.

Security! This comes in two separate forms. First, financial security is a must because you have heard the saying, "you can't live off of love." Now bringing home a paycheck is only the beginning, so don't think that the money gets you off the hook.

I'm sure you have also heard the saying that "money isn't everything." You can focus too much on finances, and come up short on the other needs your wife may have.

She needs a bodyguard for security. She likes the security of a man by her side. She doesn't want to face anything alone, otherwise she wouldn't need you.

There are some situations in which a man can handle, perhaps better than a woman. She will definitely let you know when those times come or you may see that opportunity on your own. You will learn to sense these times and be aware of your wife's coaching from the sidelines. Step up!

TIME OUT

Wake up! Open your eyes to what is going on. Are you aware that time is marching on? What are you doing with your life? You are getting older everyday and so is your wife.

Use your time wisely. It is precious. It is all you have when you think about it. One day all the sand in the top of the hourglass will be sand in the bottom. A fact is that we don't know how much sand is left for each of us.

Life should be more than a job day after day. Life should be more than just accumulating things. What are you doing with your time that will last? Are you making lots of good memories?

Are you a workaholic, always working? Haven't you heard, "Take time to stop and smell the roses"? You can finish a job or project or repair or an up-grade or addition or honey do. The work goes on and on until you come to the point in your life that... what was the point I was trying to make?

You had better do those things that make life and a marriage worthwhile. Set some goals and start the wheels in motion.

WHO'S WHO?

Hey there, what's your name? Your wife! What sweet name do you use for her? "Doll!" I have heard that name used by some husbands. Guess what, she is not a doll. Men don't play with dolls, remember? No, and don't think of her as "eye candy" either.

All women like to look nice but there is more than a pretty face there. "Babe" is also a degrading title for the woman of your life. She is a grown adult and doesn't appreciate being treated like a kid (Babe) or an object. She is a human being just as much a person as you; and as such, deserves as much (or more) respect and worth as anybody.

You probably don't mean what you call her. It's just a habit. It could be worse like, "My old lady". Better to say "My wife". Another piece of information for you, she is not your "Mom" or "Mother".

She is also not a pet, a plaything, or a sex object. This is your better half. Treat that half like you want your half treated.

Ask her how "Honey" or "Dear" sounds for a name. Oh, and what does she call you? "Bozo!"

MARRIAGE NEEDS VS. PHYSICAL NEEDS

Your body is what you make of it, and so is your marriage. To have a strong, healthy body requires some knowledge of what is good and what is not.

The same is true about marriage. The body needs the right kind of nourishment or input. Input and nourish your marriage with love, kindness, comfort, understanding, generosity, consideration, and thoughtfulness.

The body needs exercise, work and doing. Muscles tend to weaken quickly if not used often.

A good marriage uses the strength of a man (discipline, facts, courage, control) and the strength of a woman (love, social planning, and homemaking). These are general guidelines that would be found in a typical marriage.

A marriage can become weak when husband and wife are not working in unison. Pulling together, being together, eating together, sleeping together and loving together build a solid marriage. All of these are marriage exercises. A marriage requires nourishment.

After all, what was the reason to get married? It was not just to look at her…a photo would do!

HOW DO YOU RATE?

Plus vs. Minus – Positive vs. Negative. You are positive in some occasions and sometimes in a similar situation you find that you are being negative. You will not always be the best you can be. What traits are positive and which are negative?

Generous vs. Stingy – Doing your part is just the starting point. Going the extra mile, thinking of others' needs, especially the needs of your wife will pay off. You may not see this right now, but in the long run you will be noticed each time and gain some points.

Having a giving attitude will make you feel better about yourself and you will notice that no one likes a stingy person. This is one who never does his part or shares his goodies. That person is only interested in himself and his needs, desires and pleasures.

Optimist vs. Pessimist – An optimist sees things as he would like for them to be and sets reasonable goals to achieve the outcome he has hopes for. A pessimist, on the other hand, sees potential problems and tends to hold back from reaching new goals.

You be positive all the time! Remember Scrooge?

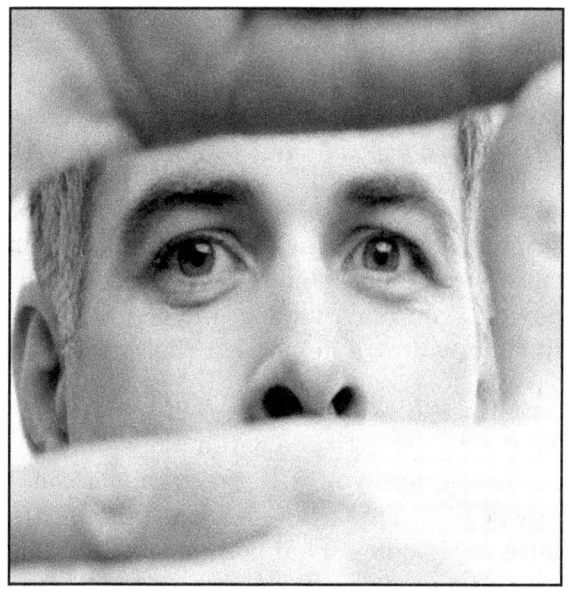

LOOKS

What fits you? What looks good on you? We aren't really talking about what size clothes you wear. The clothes don't make the man. The truth is what kind of a person you are under those expensive clothes is more important than the first impression.

A smile can show how you are feeling and looks better than a frown. Eye to eye contact shows that you are really interested in the other person. So don't be looking around when having a conversation with someone.

A touch, a wink, a hug and a kiss are all important to a wife, and you don't have to expect to go any further...just now. Play it cool and you will look cool no matter what clothes you are wearing...or not.

In conversation with others, you can look good. If a video of you was secretly made and then played back, would you be impressed with yourself? A person can look better to others when he isn't boasting and bragging on how much he is worth. People will be more impressed if you let them feel important.

Remember, "Pretty is as pretty does!"

LAYING DOWN THE LAW

Rules – Make sure you **know** what the rules are.

1. Who makes the rules?

2. Who do the rules apply to?

3. Who can break the rules?

4. What is the punishment for breaking the rules?

5. Which rules are the most important, resulting in the most severe consequences?

Rule #1 – Keep both eyes on your wife. Don't be looking around. Find out what blinders on a horse are for. Think tunnel vision. Close your eyes, turn your head.

Rule #2 – You must break and keep broken any and all past romantic relationships. This rule, if broken, carries severe penalties.

Rule #3 – This rule is a follow through to rule #1. If you happen to see another female, other than your wife, then don't let your mind think lustful thoughts. Think about something else quickly. Otherwise this could lead down the wrong path.

Look every female right in the eyes (focus on her eyes) and think of them as eyes of another guy.

Surely, you can remember only three rules….

CHANGE

What happened? Where is that woman you married? She is not the same, you say. She may look something like the person in those wedding pictures, but she seems to be a lot different than that sweet thing you dated.

Well, she may think the same thing about you too. Remember how you always tried to impress her? Are there things that you did before marriage (B.M.) that you no longer do after marriage (A.M.)?

When you start improving on your weaknesses, then you may be surprised to see that she starts making changes. But don't make the mistake of making suggestions which are critical. After all, you want to improve your marriage, not damage it.

It is always easier to point the finger and accuse her of having faults, but keep this in mind, she is human and humans are not perfect. Humans can make mistakes, but now turn the finger and point in the opposite direction.

You are human too. Before you say anything bad about your wife's taste or judgment, remember she chose you for a partner. Remember, also, when you're pointing a finger at her, three fingers are pointing back at you.

HAND IN HAND /
LOVE & TRUST

Love and trust go together in a good marriage, but either one can be broken. Marriage can be ended just on the grounds of "irreconcilable differences." What does that involve?

Well sometimes it may mean that the love fire doesn't have any more sparks. Can a marriage survive without love? Yes, but only on paper.

What about trust? It only takes one mess up to destroy years of trust and it takes a long time to put trust back together and there may still be some cracks and weaknesses. Which is most important in a marriage, love or trust?

That is not the question because they are both necessary for a good marriage. So be careful. They are both fragile and can be easily broken. Perhaps trust is more important.

Love in a marriage can slowly disappear or it can grow stronger. Trust, on the other hand can be gone in just a moment. Jealousy and suspicion can keep trust down to a low point. Trust is something you earn like respect, so be careful not to slip.

WORD MEANINGS

What do you really mean when you say, "*Honey I love you?*" This could mean that she is very desirable OR nice to have around OR I am saying this to make me some points OR just because she said it first.

Oh, no! If any of these thoughts come close to the truth then the real definition of love is not in your vocabulary. Love is not conditional on what the other person (wife) does or does not do for you. Love is not based on appearance. It is not all about you and your happiness. Love is being more concerned about your wife's happiness, needs, welfare and pleasure than your own.

Love is giving, sharing and doing for her. Love is more than words. It needs action. Love is a verb. Love and lust are two very different actions and feelings. Lust is based on looks and hormones. Love is based on concern and mutual feelings. Lust does not discriminate about who it chooses, just anybody and everybody. Love in marriage is limited to only one. Make your choice wisely.

GOOD, BAD OR NEITHER

Do you want to do right or do you want to do wrong? This question needs to apply to you just as well as your kids. In your heart you know what is right. So you know what you should or should not do.

But temptation to do wrong can be very strong. Some temptations can start out small and before you realize or can stop it, there it is – a bad habit. That bad habit can drag you down and your family suffers as well.

If you don't start these habits, you won't have to stop them. If you play with fire, you'll get burned. Bigger men than you have let their morals down and paid a high price for doing so.

"Nobody is perfect", "You owe it to yourself to try it just one time", "Come on, nobody will know", "Aren't you curious?", "Walk on the wild side", "Come on, everybody is doing it", "If it feels good, do it". Have you ever heard or even tried some of these statements? Watch out, you'll get burned!

Be sure your actions will come to public light either for right or wrong – good or bad. So be good for goodness sake.

JUGGLING

Who or what takes up most of your time? Who or what do you think about the most? Who or what is a priority in your life: job, money, kids, investments, economy, world news, politics, sports, T.V., working out, Facebook, Texting, Internet, vehicles, yard, clothes, food, friends, church???

Where does your wife rate in all these things? Stop! Before you say what you are suppose to say, take a look at your daily schedule. How much time do you devote to doing nothing else but just looking at her and talking with and listening to her?

Little moments are very important to her and will add to your close relationship. Say things like, "How are you feeling today?" or "Do you have any plans for today?" or "What would you need help with because I'm all yours!"

So don't drop the ball. Make sure everything in your life stays in the right order. Remember to really get number one to remain number one.

FARMING

Whatever you are planting is what you are going to harvest later, so make sure that you are planting the right things in your garden.

When you plant anger, don't expect to get love. You plant condemnation that is what you'll get back. Affection reaps same in good measure.

When you find something growing in your garden which you don't like, then pull it up and plant something else in its place. A good garden or marriage takes time, work, knowledge and expense, but the results are worth the effort.

Timing is very important in both farming and marriage. There is a best time to plant. When you wait too late to invest in your marriage, you may find that time has run out. *Weather* is important. Freezing cold will wipe you out. Do you get the comparison? Too much or not enough water and fertilizer can rot or dry up your plants. Are you spoiling or not appreciating your mate? Weed control is continuous or a garden can be taken over. Weeds, like problems, are easier to eliminate at an early stage.

A garden (or marriage) is a thing of beauty and something to take pride in; but you can't just plant it and leave it to take care of itself.

WEDGES AND WALLS

Don't allow the children to come between you or your wife, especially in the bed. This includes the dogs and cats even if they are part of the family. Before you know it you'll be in the doghouse.

Some things are best done in private, away from the children's ears. I'm talking about rules and discipline. What did you think I was talking about? Oh yes, that too. Children are not the only things that can come between you and your wife.

Jobs! Can you each leave your work and not bring it home with you. **Health**! It can hamper your love life so remember that and try to stay strong. Eat right and exercise for a long and loving relationship. **Hobbies**! They can be shared rather than her knitting and you in the garage. However, knitting may not work for you.

Be aware that over time, wedges can come between a husband and his wife. These things can take up time and energy, and at the end of the day, that's it. It's over and the next day is pretty much the same until the two of you are not enjoying each other's company as you would like to.

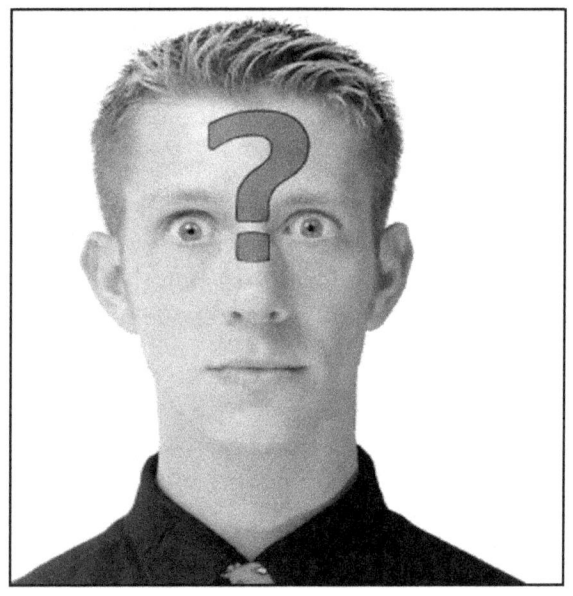

WHAT TIME IS IT?

Is it time to step up or is it time to step back? Is it your decision or hers? Is it time to state your opinion or time to keep your mouth shut? Is it time to be brave and take a risk or time to lay low?

There is always time to learn something new. You should never stop learning. Can you play a musical instrument? Can you add art to your hobbies? What about farming, horseback or motor cycle riding? The more knowledge you have, the more appeal you have with others. This includes your wife. That will pay off for some good time.

The time to decide what to do when temptation comes along is before it happens; not when. You can have your mind made up in advance. Some men think they wouldn't know until faced with crossing the lines.

Resolve in your own mind to do the right thing when the time comes and it will, perhaps more than once.

Knowing what time it is can keep you out of hot water and make you some points.

Practice saying "NO".

SIGNS

Signs! Can you read between the lines? What is she really saying? Does what she is saying or the way she is acting make any sense to you? Are you ready to throw up your hands and say, "Women! I can't understand them!"

Before you give up, first realize that you may be missing something that is right before your eyes. Do you have all the facts? Try to be a good detective. Be observant. What a person says is only part of the message.

Tone of voice, facial expressions, and body language are clues. Are you reading those? A change in attitude should and is a big clue that you may be missing something.

Most of the time you probably already know what is wrong. Did you cause it? A hurt can remain for a long time and get progressively worse. So the best time to fix a hurt is to apply "first aid" or quick healing. Forget your pride and apologize. Hurts leave scars.

You have heard perhaps of "the cold shoulder?" Well, that's a clue. There is also a "cold meal" or "eating alone". The signs you need to pay attention to are not on the TV, so put down the remote before you freeze. It can really get cold out there in the dog house!

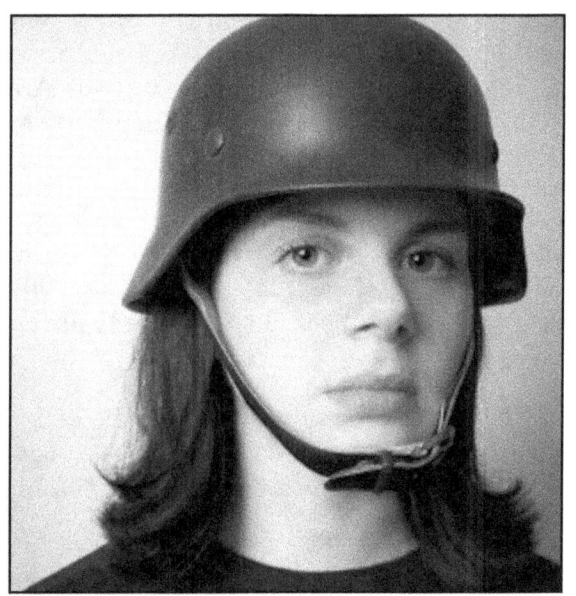

BATTLEFIELD FATIGUE

Battle, War, Enemy! This is not about seeing who wins. She is not your enemy. She is on your side. When you are feeling ready to fight someone, then look in the mirror. There is the enemy that you need to confront, not your wife. She is your helpmeet. Can you ask her to help you? You are not perfect. If you can hear what she has to say without being defensive and without being accusative of her, then you may eventually win the battle.

She won the battle when you said, "I do." You will win only when you stop fighting your partner. You won when she said, "I do." After that your chance of winning is not going to happen, so surrender and enjoy a peace accord.

The enemies that you need to face are ones which were brought into the marriage. Clean up your own act before you try to correct her. Do you have a short temper? Are you defensive, selfish, jealous, possess bad habits? Are you reclusive, or lazy? Just to mention a few.

There are also enemies coming in from outside. The internet can be a big enemy against your time and mind.

Know your enemy.

DRIVING

Just because your hands are on the steering wheel doesn't mean that you are doing the driving. There are at least two of you in the family car that is going down life's highway.

The purpose is not to see how fast you can go. The purpose is to enjoy the ride. Make some good memories from the signs along the trip. While you are aware of what's going on outside, don't forget to pay attention to those inside.

Their needs and desires are your main concern. Their safety and physical, mental, spiritual and emotional wellbeing are your responsibility.

Don't be hard-headed or too proud to ask for directions. That is not a sign of weakness. It is a sign of smarts and maturity. It never hurts to get a second opinion and be careful of trying too many shortcuts on unfamiliar routes. You could get lost in dangerous neighborhoods. Safe driving and stay out of ditches. The road ahead can be rough and smooth so choose the direction you are headed in unison with your Co-Pilot.

ABOUT THE AUTHOR

Robert E. (Bob) Bryan was born in April, 1941, the eldest of 7 siblings, in Washington, D C. After the untimely death of his father when at the age of 12 years, Bob assumed the role of "the man of the house", helping his mother raise the family. In 1959, Bob left home as a war orphan and enrolled at East Tennessee State University. He graduated with his B.S. degree four years later.

He married his wife Jo after a three year courtship. As a young married couple they relocated to Hampton, Virginia and Bob began his career teaching in the public school system at Jeff Davis Junior High School. Bob and Jo's son, Kevin, was born during the four years spent in Hampton.

The family relocated to Wilmington, North Carolina where Bob continued his teaching career at John T. Hoggard High School. Bob taught young people skills and values that prepared them for various careers including construction, engineering and NASA. His students coined the name "Daddy B" as a term of endearment. He remained at Hoggard High until his retirement in June, 1993.

The death of Bob's dad, being a formative event in his life, helped create in him the heart of a servant. He has given much of his time and talent to serving wives who found themselves in similar circumstances as did his mother in 1953. Out of this concern for widows and 48 years of marriage to Jo, along with his observation of others and the inspiration of the Lord this book emerged. The author's goal is to serve couples by helping them improve their marriage relationship and to enjoy their lives together.